INDUSTRY JOBS

JOBS IN SPORTS

BY A.W. BUCKEY

Core Library

An Imprint of Abdo Publishing
abdobooks.com

Cover image: Referees monitor sports games and make sure athletes follow the rules.

abdobooks.com

Published by Abdo Publishing, a division of ABDO, PO Box 398166, Minneapolis, Minnesota 55439.

Printed in the United States of America, North Mankato, Minnesota.
052023
092023

THIS BOOK CONTAINS RECYCLED MATERIALS

Cover Photo: Don Juan Moore/Getty Images Sport/Getty Images
Interior Photos: Dustin Bradford/Icon Sportswire/Getty Images, 4–5, 42 (top); Mark Blinch/NHLI/Getty Images, 7; Marvin Ibo Guengoer/GES Sportfoto/Getty Images Sport/Getty Images, 10–11, 42 (top middle); Red Line Editorial, 12; Takuya Matsumoto/The Yomiuri Shimbun/AP Images, 13; Bryan Bedder/Getty Images for IMG/Getty Images Entertainment/Getty Images, 15; Cedric Ribeiro/Getty Images Entertainment/Getty Images, 18; Rusty Jones/AP Images, 22–23, 42 (middle); Rebecca Blackwell/AP Images, 25, 42 (bottom middle); Gia Quilap/SPP/Sipa USA/AP Images, 27, 42 (bottom); Nick Wass/AP Images, 28–29, 43 (top), 45; Shutterstock Images, 31 (top left, bottom middle left), 31 (top middle left), 31 (top middle right, top right), 31 (bottom left, bottom middle right, bottom right); Jane Tyska/Digital First Media/East Bay Times/MediaNews Group/Getty Images, 32, 43 (top middle); Branislav Nenin/Shutterstock Images, 36–37, 43 (bottom middle); Dima Sidelnikov/iStockphoto, 38, 43 (bottom); Jeff Chiu/AP Images, 41, 43 (middle)

Editor: Laura Stickney
Series Designer: Katharine Hale

Library of Congress Control Number: 2022949097

Publisher's Cataloging-in-Publication Data

Names: Buckey, A. W., author.
Title: Jobs in sports / by A. W. Buckey
Description: Minneapolis, Minnesota: Abdo Publishing Company, 2024 | Series: Industry jobs | Includes online resources and index.
Identifiers: ISBN 9781098290894 (lib. bdg.) | ISBN 9781098277079 (ebook)
Subjects: LCSH: Occupations--Juvenile literature. | Sports--Biography--Juvenile literature. | Sports personnel--Biography--Juvenile literature.
Classification: DDC 796.023--dc23

CONTENTS

BALL ARENA
Ball
LIGHTNING
AVALANCHE
BLOCKS
HITS
FACEOFF %
SAVE %
VS.
0
3:32
1ST
SOG
2022 PLAYOFFS
HONDA
abc
Great Clips
Jägermeister
DRAFTKINGS SPORTSBOOK
adiclub
DISCOVER
Expedia
Made to Travel
pepsi
ZERO SUGAR
TOYOTA
BALL ARENA

CHAPTER ONE

MELTING THE ICE

Lauren unlocks the doors to the hockey arena at 7:00 a.m. and steps inside. That evening, the venue will host nearly 20,000 people. There will be yelling, cheering, and the swoosh of skates. But for now, the arena is quiet.

Lauren begins cleaning the protective glass around the hockey rink. Soon other staff members join her. They discuss the day's schedule. The hockey rink must be ready when the team arrives. The workers clean spots

Some ice technicians drive Zamboni machines on indoor stadium rinks used by professional athletes. Others work on outdoor rinks meant for public skating.

SPORTS WITH ICE RESURFACERS

Hockey isn't the only sport that requires smooth, well-maintained ice. Figure skaters and speed skaters also need ice resurfacer machine drivers on their rinks. Each sport has different ice requirements. For example, figure skaters need warmer, thicker ice than speed skaters. This is so their skates can dig into the ice, which makes it easier to perform jumps.

off the ice by hand. Then Lauren gives the rink its first daily cleaning with the ice resurfacing machine, or Zamboni.

Lauren's official title is ice technician. But she likes the name that some people at the stadium call her. During breaks in a game, Lauren gets on the ice resurfacing machine and drives onto the rink. Kids always call out, "It's the Zamboni driver!" When she hears them, Lauren smiles and waves.

The name Zamboni comes from the machine's inventor, Frank J. Zamboni. The Zamboni machine looks like a small truck with a mop-like attachment in back. It shaves off the top layer of ice on the rink. Then it

When ice technicians aren't driving the Zamboni, they may help perform routine maintenance and clean parts of the stadium.

rinses the surface of the ice to clean off dirt. Finally, it leaves a layer of clean water that freezes into new ice. In a professional hockey rink, the ice must be kept at a certain thickness and temperature. If the ice is too warm, it could melt. If the ice is too thick, it becomes difficult to maintain. During a game, Lauren drives the Zamboni machine around the rink several times, traveling a total of 3 miles (4.8 km). It's an important job. The hockey players need smooth ice to play on!

Lauren loves being inside hockey arenas. Some of her happiest memories are attending hockey games with her family. Lauren also played hockey throughout

PERSPECTIVES

FEMALE ICE RESURFACER DRIVERS

Most ice resurfacer drivers are men. But more women have started doing this job. Alison Murdock was the first full-time female Zamboni driver in the National Hockey League (NHL). She started working for the Tampa Bay Lightning in the late 2010s. In 2019, Canadian Joanne Kuzoff also began driving the Zamboni for NHL games. Kuzoff enjoys representing women in the hockey business. "It is nice to do what I love and to represent that it doesn't matter if you are a male or a female," Kuzoff says. "[Ice resurfacing] can be a boys club, but it doesn't have to be."

high school and college. She studied business management. She liked being part of a team and helping projects run smoothly. One summer, Lauren was an intern in a professional hockey team's business office. She talked to the team's ice technician. Lauren saw how much he liked his job. He got to go to games and work with others. Lauren knew then that ice technician was the job for her. She loves being able to work in hockey. After all these years, she's still part of the game.

THE WORLD OF SPORTS

Lauren is one of many people who work in the world of sports. The sports world includes more than just athletes. Workers like Lauren make it possible for sports games to happen. Maintenance workers and concessions workers help out at games too. People who coach and train athletes are also important. They may work with professionals, students, or children, providing physical and mental support.

Other workers report on sports, helping fans learn more about games and athletes. Professional sports is a big business. In North America, the sports industry earns about $70 billion every year. Workers gather important information about sports and keep sports businesses running. They also buy and sell things, such as merchandise and advertising.

These workers all play important roles in the sports business. They help the world of sports run smoothly and efficiently. They make it possible for fans to enjoy games and events worldwide.

FIFA
AFA

CHAPTER TWO

PROFESSIONAL ATHLETES

Professional athletes make money by playing sports. They compete in games and competitions. People attend these events or follow them through the media. For example, professional soccer players join teams and play in games that people watch. Professional swimmers compete in swim meets that are open to spectators.

Athletes make a living by using their skills for entertainment. They can earn money in different ways. Some athletes who join

Professional athletes compete in leagues. Sometimes they compete in tournaments, such as the FIFA World Cup. Soccer star Lionel Messi helped his team win the World Cup in 2022.

AVERAGE US PROFESSIONAL SPORTS SALARIES, 2019–2020

Sport	Male Athletes	Female Athletes
Basketball	$8,321,937	$75,181
Golf	$1,235,495	$48,993
Soccer	$410,730	$35,000
Baseball/Softball	$4,031,549	$6,000
Tennis	$335,946	$283,635

Male professional athletes often have much higher salaries than female professional athletes. Why do you think this pay gap exists? What could be done to make sure female athletes receive equal pay?

professional teams are paid a salary, or regular sum of money. They sign contracts, or legal documents that state how much they'll be paid. For in-demand athletes, salaries can be very high. However, female professional athletes make less money than male athletes. In the 2022–2023 basketball season, male players in the National Basketball Association (NBA) had an average salary of more than $9.37 million. But female players in

One of the most famous sports tournaments is the Wimbledon Championships, an annual tennis tournament held in the United Kingdom. Many people, such as ball boys and girls, are needed to help prepare the tennis courts and assist during matches.

the Women's National Basketball Association (WNBA) made an average salary of only $102,750.

While athletes' salaries can be high, their careers are often short. Professional sports are hard on the body. It is difficult to stay in peak physical shape. The average National Football League (NFL) player retires at about age 28. In other industries, most people work until they are in their 60s.

Many professional athletes do not make salaries. They make money from competitions and tournaments. They play alone or in pairs, earning prize money from sports events. Many marathon races have cash prizes for the top finishers. The Professional Golf Association (PGA) hosts a yearly tour, or series of tournaments. The tour includes competitions that offer a purse, or total amount of money split between participants. The top golfer wins the most money from the purse, then the second-place golfer, and so on.

ESPORTS PROFESSIONALS

Electronic sports, or esports, are video games played in competitions. These games may or may not be about traditional sports. Esports players sign up for intense live competitions against other video game players. Esports games are often played in large arenas. Like traditional sports athletes, professional esports players can win money at these tournaments.

More than 850 athletes have graced the iconic Wheaties cereal box. Tennis star Serena Williams, who was featured in 2019, said of the achievement, "I have dreamt of this."

Professional athletes also make money from sponsorships and endorsements. Sponsorships are payments that athletes receive from people or companies. Tennis champion Naomi Osaka earns money from her partnerships with more than 20 companies, such as Nike. Companies may also sponsor athletes in exchange for endorsements. An endorsement is a stamp of approval for a product. Endorsements often appear in the form of advertising.

One of the most famous examples of athletic endorsements is the Wheaties cereal box. The General

Mills company advertises Wheaties as the "Breakfast of Champions." Famous athletes like Olympic gymnast Simone Biles are paid to have their photos on the front of the cereal box.

Advertising dollars can support athletes in other ways. For example, Adidas might pay a soccer player to wear their shoes during games. Companies also pay NASCAR teams to put their logos on their race cars.

MAINTAINING A CAREER

Athletes do not need college degrees to play professionally. Instead, they prepare for their careers through years of coaching and training. This training often takes place in the world of amateur sports, such as college sports. People who play sports without payment are called amateur athletes. It's sometimes hard to tell the difference between professionals and amateurs. Many skilled college athletes receive scholarships or free college tuition. But they are not considered professional athletes because they usually don't get paid. However, some amateur athletes are now able to do endorsements.

Very few people become professional athletes. In 2021, about 16,000 people in the United States worked as professional athletes. That is only about .005 percent of the US population.

The most successful professional athletes can make a lot of money. But many professionals struggle to maintain their careers. Maintaining an

PERSPECTIVES

WORKING ABROAD

Many US basketball players find jobs playing in overseas basketball leagues. In the 2021–2022 basketball off-season, many WNBA players played in countries such as China, Australia, and France. Some female players can earn 10 times their US salary in other countries. They sometimes enjoy perks like luxury hotels. But it can be difficult for athletes to play professionally year-round. Navigating unfamiliar countries can be hard. "Players are expected to play under any circumstances imaginable," says experienced overseas player Jose Colorado. He says players must be ready to quickly adapt to new teams and different styles of gameplay.

Many athletes work side jobs to support their sports careers. Others start their own businesses to plan for life after retirement. Russian tennis star Maria Sharapova, for example, started a candy company.

athletic career requires much more than talent. Athletes must have motivation and mental strength. They must deal with disappointment gracefully and interact with many people. Professional athletes must also manage their finances carefully. They must spend money to increase their chances of success, while planning for a future after their sports career ends.

A professional athlete's career comes with costs such as coaching and travel. Lower-level professional athletes sometimes struggle to make enough money to pay for these costs. For example, the average professional female golfer made around $49,000 in 2019. The average professional softball player made just $6,000. Professional athletes who make low salaries cannot afford to hire staff members such as personal trainers. They often work other jobs to make ends meet. Softball player Cat Osterman retired in 2021 after winning three Olympic medals. Starting in 2008, however, she balanced her professional softball career by working as an assistant coach at a college.

OTHER JOB OPPORTUNITIES

Some professional athletes choose careers outside of sports, including jobs in the world of entertainment.

Disney on Ice, for instance, is a traveling show that features Disney characters, music, and stories. Trained figure skaters act out these stories on the ice rink, using jumps and tricks.

Other professional athletes become stunt performers. These people do dangerous tricks, such as falling from buildings. These athletes often come from contact sports such as football and mixed martial arts. Their physical strength and discipline help them perform extreme stunts.

STRAIGHT TO THE SOURCE

College athletes train and play in games. In some cases, they make money for their universities. Yet they are not paid like professional athletes. Some people believe college athletes should not be paid:

> *Almost all college athletes get scholarship money to play for a university. If you consider athletes who get full rides, instead of paying 100 grand, they pay absolutely nothing. Most people would agree that these college athletes are already getting paid!*
>
> *These college athletes also get free food on their meal plans. Players also get free housing on campus with teammates that is completely paid for. . . .*
>
> *College is meant for students to learn. It is not a job. It is not meant for student athletes to get paid.*

Source: Megan James. "NCAA: Why College Athletes Should NOT Be Paid." *Medium*, 3 Nov. 2019, medium.com. Accessed 16 Nov. 2022.

CHANGING MINDS

Take a position on paying college athletes, then imagine that your best friend has the opposite opinion. Write a short essay trying to change your friend's mind. Include facts and details that support your opinion.

CHAPTER THREE

COACHES, TRAINERS, AND MEDICAL PROFESSIONALS

Athletes of all levels need people to help them prepare for competitions and improve their skills. They also need people to help them stay healthy. Scouts, coaches, trainers, and medical professionals provide the support that athletes need.

Scouts look for athletes with the ability to play at top levels. For example, a college baseball scout will attend high school baseball games. There, the scout searches for players

Sports coaches help keep their teams motivated and focused during games. They also plan game strategies and lead team practices.

PERSPECTIVES

COACHING ATHLETES WITH DISABILITIES

Some coaches specialize in helping athletes with disabilities. These athletes may have unique physical, mental, and emotional needs. Good coaches adapt their teaching and training to athletes' unique needs. Karate coach André Langevin runs a dojo, or karate school, for autistic people. Martial arts can be beneficial for autistic people. The sport helps develop coordination and mental calm. But some autistic people struggle with the pace and instructions of traditional classes. Langevin takes a flexible approach to training his students. "You need to adapt, especially for the beginners," he says.

who might be a good fit for college baseball teams.

Coaches teach and train athletes. They design practices and drills to help athletes hone their skills. They also give feedback on athletes' performances. Some coaches train professional athletes, while others work in schools and colleges. Coaches are experts in their sport of choice. They know what good athletic performance looks like. In 2021, 244,300 coaches and

Trainers often help athletes stretch before games and practices. They also provide first aid to athletes who get injured while playing.

scouts worked in the United States. The number of coaches and scouts is expected to grow by 2031.

Coaches who work in schools and colleges usually need bachelor's degrees. Many choose college majors such as sports management. Coaches must also have strong management and communication skills. Many coaches are former athletes, but they don't have to be. Some teams also hire strength and conditioning coaches, who focus on athletes' overall physical shape.

ATHLETIC TRAINERS AND SPORTS MEDICINE PROFESSIONALS

All athletes need health care. When injuries happen, athletes need help healing and getting back into shape.

People who work in sports health care help treat injured athletes.

Athletic trainers treat athletes' injuries and make recovery plans. A recovery plan might involve a period of rest, followed by a series of exercises. Most trainers get bachelor's or master's degrees, along with certification from the National Athletic Trainers' Association (NATA). Athletic trainers keep track of athletes' needs and progress. They must know how to treat common injuries and communicate well with others.

Nurses and doctors can also specialize in the field

SPORTS PSYCHOLOGY

Psychology is the study of how people think and act. Sports psychology focuses on the mental and emotional aspects of sports. Sports psychologists help individuals or groups. For example, an athlete who fears crowds might struggle at competitions. A sports psychologist can help the athlete work through his or her fears. Sports psychologists also work with teams to help team members communicate better.

Team physicians help keep track of athletes' health. They attend team games to assess and treat any injuries that occur.

of sports medicine. Some work as team physicians, taking care of team members. Orthopedic medicine, or the medicine of muscles and bones, also has a sports medicine specialty. Sports medicine orthopedists treat athletes for breaks, sprains, and dislocations.

EXPLORE ONLINE

Chapter Three discusses sports coaches. The website below describes some of the characteristics of a great coach. How does the information from the website add to what you learned in the chapter? Did it answer any of the questions you had about coaches?

QUALITIES OF A GREAT SPORTS COACH

abdocorelibrary.com/jobs-in-sports

CHAPTER FOUR

SUPPORT AND MAINTENANCE STAFF

Sports games can't exist without a lot of help. Athletes need food, uniforms, and places to play. Coaches and trainers need space and equipment. And people who come to sports events need food, drinks, shelter, and safety. This is where support and maintenance workers come in.

Most sports take place in fields, pools, courts, and gymnasiums. Maintenance professionals, such as ice technicians, keep these sports venues clean and safe.

Groundskeepers are responsible for watering and mowing the grass in sports venues.

OLYMPICS SUPPORT STAFF

The Olympic Games take place every four years in a different location. Many cities build new facilities for the Olympics. These new stadiums, pools, rinks, and arenas need lots of temporary staff. Often, these people work for free in exchange for access to events. More than 70,000 people volunteered as staff for the 2020 Tokyo Olympics.

Their jobs may include maintenance work such as sweeping and mopping. They may also require special skills. For example, groundskeepers are people who maintain landscapes such as lawns and gardens. They work in sports venues, including grass tennis courts, golf courses, and baseball fields. Groundskeepers often get college degrees in agriculture, which involves farming. Then they specialize in growing and maintaining grass for sports fields. The job requires math and science skills. For example, Baltimore Orioles groundskeeper Nicole Sherry keeps track of the temperature of the field's soil. She pays close attention to the weather and the amount of

WORKERS AT WIMBLEDON

Thousands of people come together to make the yearly tennis tournament in Wimbledon a success. They include about 3,000 concessions workers, as well as hundreds of umpires, court attendants, and ball boys and girls. Why do you think it's important to have these workers at the event? What would happen if there were no support workers?

water in the soil. She must cover the grass when it rains because soggy grounds are too difficult to play on.

CONCESSIONS AND SECURITY

When it's time for a sports game, many people come together to help fans. Sporting events need people to sell and take tickets. They need staff to sell concessions, or food, drinks, and other items. These workers usually

Concessions workers, such as Hal the Hot Dog Guy, *left*, might sell foods like hot dogs, cotton candy, and French fries at sports games.

receive on-the-job training and need strong customer service skills. They must solve problems quickly, empathize with others, and talk with many people. They help create a fun, positive atmosphere. Concessions workers can even become beloved entertainers. In the United States, for instance, hot dogs are a traditional baseball game food. Hot dog sellers walk up and down the bleachers selling hot dogs. Some, like Hal the Hot Dog Guy, joke and talk with fans. Hal works at the Oakland Coliseum in Oakland, California. He sells hot dogs during Oakland Athletics baseball games. Hal even has his own baseball cards.

At sports events, security guards make sure that fans stay safe and follow the rules. Maintenance staff take care of lighting, music, and electricity for scoreboards. Sports competitions also need judges, scorekeepers,

PERSPECTIVES

STADIUM SECURITY

The sports world gives people chances to explore jobs they might not have considered. Liz S. found a job as a security guard at Gillette Stadium in Massachusetts. Liz had no background in security but was curious about part-time work. Liz traveled around the stadium during games. Her shifts usually lasted eight to ten hours, from five hours before the game to one hour afterward. She talked to people who broke rules, such as the smoking ban. Liz came to enjoy the job. "In the end, if you are a sports fan it is pretty cool to say you work at the stadium," she said.

and umpires. These people know the rules of the sport. Judges work in sports such as gymnastics and figure skating. Scorekeepers keep track of which team is winning, while umpires make sure players follow game rules.

TEAM CHEFS

Support staff also meet the needs of athletes and coaches. Team chefs cook and prepare food for team members. They must balance athletes' need for energy and nutrition with other concerns.

For example, NBA players are famous for their love of peanut butter and jelly sandwiches. These sandwiches are packed with sugar and protein for quick energy. Team chefs prepare many sandwiches for the players. In 2017, Milwaukee Bucks chef Shawn Zell guessed that he made between 20 and 30 sandwiches every day for players.

STRAIGHT TO THE SOURCE

Sport New Zealand is the governing body for sports in that country. It stresses the importance of sports officials:

> *Being an official is an extremely important role in any sport. Without officials giving up their time, most sporting competitions would be unable to function. Officiating can be challenging, and unfortunately some officials are subjected to hostile behavior by participants, spectators and others.*
>
> *Officials need to ensure that their approach towards officiating is in line with the aims of the competition; for example, junior competitions are usually aimed at fun and skill development rather than winning. Officials should be aware that their approach to officiating can influence the participants' experience and enjoyment of the sport.*

Source: "Roles of Officials." *Sport New Zealand*, 20 May 2014, sportnz.org.nz. Accessed 16 Nov. 2022.

BACK IT UP

The author of this passage is using evidence to support a point. Write a paragraph describing the point the author is making. Then write down two or three pieces of evidence the author uses to make the point.

CHAPTER FIVE

SPORTS BUSINESS AND SPORTS MEDIA

The world of professional sports is also a business. Professional sports teams are companies owned by very wealthy people. The teams exist to make money. Professional sports teams must pay athletes, coaches, and support staff. To make money, sports teams sell tickets to games and events. They also sell merchandise, such as sweatshirts and toys. Many teams also sell advertising. Spaces in stadiums, gyms,

Business development managers assist sports teams with marketing, business deals, and contract negotiations.

Sports data analysts might collect information about athletes' performances and gameplay strategies. They may also study fan data, such as social media engagement.

rinks, and other sports venues can be covered with company advertisements.

Business executives are responsible for managing teams and making a profit, or money beyond what's needed to pay bills. Business development managers help teams find new paths to money and success. For example, a business development manager for a hockey team might work with companies that advertise at the rink. The manager tries to get ads for a good price.

Business development managers might also work with sports data analysts, who gather information about games, players, and teams. They use math and statistics to interpret the results. Data about athletes' performances may be used to help guide team hiring decisions. Sports data analysts must understand business and sports. They must also be good at working with others and multitasking. Most sports management careers require a bachelor's degree.

SPORTS JOURNALISM

Some people work in sports media, or the world of sports news. Sportswriters or sports journalists report on sports. They work for newspapers, magazines, websites, TV, radio, or podcasts. Sports journalists might discuss games as they happen or interview

ANNOUNCERS AND COMMENTATORS

Before television, people listened to sports games on the radio. Radio announcers gave a play-by-play of a game, describing the actions of the game out loud. Their job was to make the game exciting to people who could not see it. Some people still do this job. Eventually, a second person began adding color commentary on game broadcasts. The color commentator adds interesting facts about the game and players.

PERSPECTIVES

INTERVIEWING ATHLETES

Sports media professionals interview athletes before, after, and sometimes during games. A good sports interviewer must be knowledgeable about the subject. Alex Flanagan is a sideline reporter. This role involves gathering information for the TV audience and sometimes interviewing players or coaches. Flanagan must be well prepared. Before interviewing a team, she researches the players and any new developments in the team. "I would read hundreds of clippings each week sent to me by the team's media department," Flanagan says. Flanagan's research helps her ask important questions.

athletes after games. They must have strong communication skills and a deep knowledge of their topic.

Some professional athletes find second careers in sports media. After retiring from playing, they work as sports commentators and broadcasters. Former professional soccer player Aly Wagner retired in 2010. She now works as a soccer commentator and analyst.

The sports world provides people with

Some sports reporters cover live sports events. They attend games, interview athletes and coaches, and report on recent team developments.

many exciting career options. Few people become professional athletes, but many people work together to make sports events possible. People who are passionate about sports can discover and pursue exciting and challenging careers.

FURTHER EVIDENCE

Chapter Five covers the sports media business. What was one of the main points of this chapter? What evidence is included to support this point? Read the article at the website below. Does the information on the website support the main point of the chapter? Does it present new evidence?

WHAT IS SPORTS JOURNALISM?

abdocorelibrary.com/jobs-in-sports

JOB LIST

Ice technicians clean and prepare rinks for ice-based sports.

Professional athletes play sports for money.

Coaches lead sports teams and help athletes improve their skills.

Athletic trainers treat muscle and bone injuries. They help injured athletes recover.

Team physicians are doctors who work for sports teams.

Groundskeepers maintain fields or grass on sports fields.

Concessions stand workers sell food or drinks at sports events.

Sports journalists are writers and reporters who cover sports news.

Business development coordinators help grow a sports business.

Sports data analysts review data from sports games and businesses and use it to make decisions.

STOP AND THINK

Dig Deeper

After reading this book, what questions do you still have about jobs in sports media? With an adult's help, find a few reliable sources that can help you answer your questions. Write a paragraph about what you learned.

Another View

Chapter Two talks about what life can be like for professional athletes. As you know, every source is different. Ask a librarian or another adult to help you find another source about working as an athlete. What is the point of view of each author? How are they similar and why? How are they different and why?

Take a Stand

Some people believe that college athletes should get salaries. Other people think that college athletes are compensated in other ways, such as scholarships. What is your point of view? Do you think college athletes should be paid? Use evidence to support your ideas.

Tell the Tale

Chapter Four of this book discusses how groundskeepers do their jobs. Imagine you are a groundskeeper for a baseball team. What do you see, smell, and hear when you go to work? What does your day look like?

GLOSSARY

advertising
messages that encourage people to buy a product or service

broadcast
a TV, radio, or internet transmission of an event

commentator
a person who talks about a sports event as it happens

contact sport
a sport that leads to physical contact and touch between players

executive
a manager and decision maker in a business

intern
a trainee at a workplace who is learning about a job or business

marathon
a running race of 26.2 miles (42 km)

spectator
a person who watches at a sports game, show, or event

tournament
a series of competitions that lead to an overall winner

venue
a place where an event is held

ONLINE RESOURCES

To learn more about jobs in sports, visit our free resource websites below.

Core Library CONNECTION
FREE! COMMON CORE MULTIMEDIA RESOURCES

Visit **abdocorelibrary.com** or scan this QR code for free Common Core resources for teachers and students, including vetted activities, multimedia, and booklinks, for deeper subject comprehension.

Booklinks NONFICTION NETWORK
FREE! ONLINE NONFICTION RESOURCES

Visit **abdobooklinks.com** or scan this QR code for free additional online weblinks for further learning. These links are routinely monitored and updated to provide the most current information available.

LEARN MORE

Dakers, Diane. *Sports Journalism*. Crabtree, 2018.

Davidson, B. Keith. *WNBA*. Crabtree, 2022.

Martin, Steve. *I Like Sports . . . What Jobs Are There?* Kane Miller, 2020.

INDEX

About the Author

A.W. Buckey is a writer living in Brooklyn, New York. She is a fan of the Brooklyn Cyclones professional baseball team.